CIVILIZATION'S DRYING CRADLE- WATER POLITICS IN THE TIGRIS-EUPHRATES RIVER BASIN

> Too often, where we need water, we find guns....As the global economy grows, so will its thirst....Many more conflicts lie over the horizon.
>
> —UN Secretary General Ban Ki-moon[1]

Limited freshwater supplies, population growth, and chronic pollution will ensure that water disputes increasingly shape Middle East politics for the foreseeable future. Exacerbating the water supply problem is the fact that all three of the Middle East's major river basins, the Nile, Jordan, and Tigris-Euphrates, are shared by four or more countries. Since 1953 the United States has attempted to mediate Jordan River water-negotiations between Israel, Jordan, Lebanon, and Syria, and the 1967 Six-Day War was in part a war over water access in the Jordan River basin.[2] During 1974-1975 and again in 1990, Iraq threatened to go to war with its neighbors over access to Euphrates River flows.[3] In 1992 one writer asserted that, "over the next decade, water issues in the three major river basins will foster an unprecedented degree of co-operation or a combustible level of conflict."[4]

Despite worsening water availability and equity in the Tigris-Euphrates river basin, a military conflict over water is unlikely while Iraq and Syria remain militarily, politically, and economically weaker than Turkey.[5] However the potential for downstream crisis, human suffering, and conflict will only increase as Turkey continues work on the Southeast Anatolia Development Project (GAP), which includes 22 dams and 19 hydroelectric plants. These dams will provide Turkey with unprecedented control over both Tigris and Euphrates River flows into Syria and Iraq. From its position of strength, Turkey is unlikely to make meaningful concessions on water sharing without application of significant external diplomatic pressure, economic incentives, and concessions from Syria and Iraq. Although near-term military conflict in the Tigris-Euphrates river basin over water is unlikely, regional water shortages and inequities will increasingly challenge U.S. interests, and with international water law and organizations unlikely to resolve Turkish, Syrian, and Iraqi differences, a long-term water-sharing treaty, facilitated by external influence, is needed. The United States has an opportunity to use diplomacy and incentives to move Turkey, Syria, and Iraq toward a long term water-sharing agreement, to promote regional stability and the political and economic viability of the three countries.

In order to illustrate the importance of water scarcity for Middle East politics, this paper describes the challenging political and economic relationships between Turkey, Syria, and Iraq that will continue to be heavily influenced by the availability and access to water of the Tigris and Euphrates rivers. This paper outlines the challenges to reaching water-sharing agreements between riparian nations, and analyzes why developing international water laws and conventions are inadequate to meet the challenges of projected water shortages. It draws parallels between the riparian countries of the Tigris-Euphrates basin and the relationships between riparian nations of the Jordan and Nile River basins, and offers insight towards future potential water sharing agreements by looking at the Colorado River treaty between the United States and Mexico. This paper will outline United States policy options in the region and assess the risks and opportunities associated with these options. Finally, the paper will examine the feasibility of developing alternative water sources, and the critical need to improve utilization and management of existing water resources, particularly in Iraq.

Borders and Water Imbalance in the Tigris-Euphrates River Basin

The geography and hydrology of the Tigris-Euphrates river basin and the competing water needs of Turkey, Syria, and Iraq make competition and conflict over the basin's water resources inevitable. The headwaters for both rivers rise almost entirely in the mountains of Turkey's East Anatolia region, fed by snowmelt and spring rains. The Khabur River in Syria adds just 5% to the Euphrates' flow, and there are no additions in Iraq.[6] Flowing over 2700 km through Turkey, Syria, and Iraq the Euphrates joins the Tigris River at the Shatt al-Arab for a final 200 km before entering the Persian Gulf [see map, Figure 1]. The Tigris River flows 400 km through Turkey, forms the border between Syria and Turkey for 44 km, then crosses into Iraq. The Tigris' principal tributary, the Greater Zab, originates in Turkey's Taurus mountains and flows independently into Iraq before joining the Tigris south of Mosul. Flowing for 1400 km through Iraq, the Tigris is joined by the Lesser Zab and Diyala Rivers flowing out of Iran, and the Adhaim River, which flows intermittently and makes a minor contribution from a catchment totally in Iraq.[7]

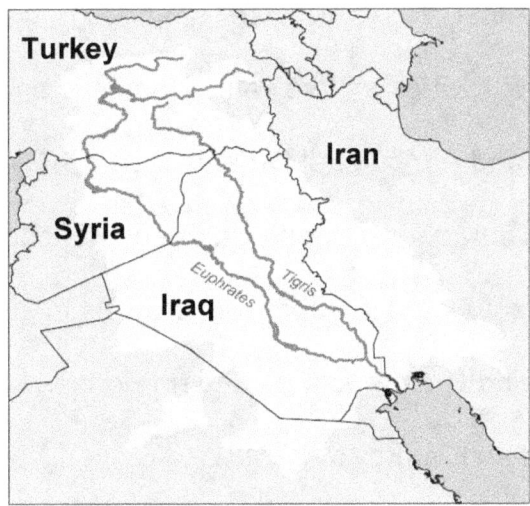

Figure 1. Tigris-Euphrates River basin

Turkey's average rainfall is more than twice that of Syria, and nearly three times Iraq's, thus while both the Tigris and Euphrates are largely sourced in Turkey, the demand and need for the water is greatest in Syria and Iraq, with Iraq's position most vulnerable as the furthest downstream riparian.[8] The flow of both rivers is seasonal, peaking in April-May and ebbing in August-September, and highly-variable between years of drought or floods. Prior to construction of large dams on the Euphrates in the 1970s by Turkey and Syria, the average annual flow into Iraq was 33 km^3, and the flow of the Tigris was a third larger, at 48 km^3 annually.[9] However the annual flows of both rivers may vary considerably, which has been a significant obstacle in defining guaranteed downstream flows for Syria and Iraq in water negotiations with Turkey.

The growing populations and agricultural demands of Turkey, Syria, and Iraq combine to place maximum strain on the region's water resources, but there are differences in each country's water needs and uses. Iraq's population of 31 million is less than half of Turkey's 72 million, but it is growing nearly twice as fast, while Syria's smaller population of 21 million has the slowest growth.[10] Iraq's groundwater resources are extremely limited, less than 1/20th of Turkey's, and 1/14th of Syria's, making Iraq highly-dependent on surface water withdrawals. Domestic and agricultural water use data tracked by the Food and Agricultural Organization (FAO) of the United Nations from 2000-2003 shows that Iraq's per capita water consumption was three times greater than Turkey's, and Iraq's estimated irrigation withdrawals in 2000 greatly exceeded Turkey's, despite Iraq having fewer hectares under irrigation. Syria's per capita water consumption was twice that of Turkey's.[11] Iraq and Syria's water consumption is

4

frequently criticized as wasteful and mismanaged when Turkey responds to demands that it pass more water through its Euphrates River reservoirs.[12]

<u>Dam Builders and Water Diversion</u>

The Southeast Anatolia Development Project (Turkish- *Güneydoğu Anadolu Projesi,* GAP) is a $36-billion, multi-sector development project that aims to raise income and living standards in nine of Turkey's poorest and least developed provinces located in the Tigris and Euphrates upper basins, while providing national hydroelectric power and growth for the agricultural sector. The GAP master plan includes 22 dams and 19 hydroelectric power stations, with 14 dams on the Euphrates River and its tributaries, and 8 dams on the Tigris and its tributaries. As of 2011, a total of fifteen dams were complete, including six large dams on the Euphrates and three on tributaries of the Tigris.[13] Ataturk Dam, the largest dam on the Euphrates and world's 5th largest in volume, was completed in 1990 and its reservoir was filled by 1992. Water from this reservoir is diverted through the Sanliurfa tunnel system, consisting of twin 25-foot diameter tunnels that are 16.4 miles long, and capable of diverting 328 m^3/s to irrigation, representing one-third of the Euphrates River flow. This water now irrigates up to 4760 km^2 in the Harran and Mardin-Ceylanpinar plains.[14] Crops in this formerly arid land are 90 percent cotton, and with a 150 percent increase in planted acreage since 1995, Turkey ranked 7th in worldwide cotton production in 2007.[15]

The decrease of Euphrates River flows into Syria and Iraq from the Ataturk Dam and other GAP projects have been significant, and during drought years, disastrous. Prior to 1970, Iraq received an average 33 km^3 of water annually in the Euphrates River. As impoundments and diversions of water by the Ataturk and other dams increased, flow has been reduced over 70%, to as little as 8 km^3 annually.[16] In a

5

bilateral agreement with Syria, Turkey has promised to preserve Euphrates flow at the Turkish-Syrian border at 500 m^3/s (15.4 km^3/yr), however Syria has accused Turkey of not maintaining this flow during drought periods.[17] Syria's three dams on the Euphrates also control flow into Iraq, particularly the Tabqa Dam which impounds Lake Assad. Since 1975 Syria has agreed to pass 60% of the Euphrates flow it receives from Turkey on to Iraq, leaving Iraq approximately 9 km^3 of Euphrates River flow in an average year, subject to releases from Turkey into Syria.[18] With its access to Euphrates flows marginalized, Iraqi dependency on the Tigris River has increased, however three large Turkish dams on the Tigris are under construction and scheduled for completion by 2015. The most controversial of these is the Ilisu Dam, which will impound a 313 km^2 reservoir and flood over 185 Kurdish villages and hamlets, displacing up to 55,000 people.[19] Iraqis now fear a reduction of Tigris river flows similar to the demise of the Euphrates.

The Peril of Irrigation

Irrigation's significant benefits and harmful effects make it an unavoidable paradox for arid Middle East countries and the Tigris-Euphrates basin in particular. Vital to the world's food supply, irrigated agriculture enables 40 percent of the world's food production on just 16 percent of its arable land, and in the Middle East, 70 percent of agriculture production comes from irrigated land.[20] While the need for irrigated agriculture is great, its productivity exacts tremendous tolls in water withdrawals, damaged land, and polluted watersheds. One hectare of irrigated land requires an average of 12,000 m^3 water annually.[21] Irrigation accounts for nearly 88 percent of Syria's freshwater withdrawals, with Iraq and Turkey following close behind at 80 percent and 74 percent respectively.[22] Additionally, salt inevitably accumulates in

6

irrigated soils through evaporation of frequently applied water, and upward leaching of salts already present in the water table. The problem is exacerbated by outdated flooding irrigation techniques that are less than 50 percent efficient, overwatering crops with insufficient drainage to allow runoff to remove the excess salts.[23] Even when fields are properly drained in flood irrigation, the runoff is usually five times as salty as the inflow. Thus the problem worsens progressively as downstream farmers and communities are forced to use polluted runoff from upstream irrigation projects, already highly saline and contaminated with herbicides. Soil salinization is particularly acute in southern Iraq, where the existing water table is saline and close enough to the surface that even a limited over-application of irrigation water will raise salts to root-level and destroy the crop. As a result, 74% of the arable land in Iraq has a harmful degree of salinity.[24] Worldwide, acute salinization removes an estimated 2 percent of previously irrigated land from agriculture annually, and it can only be remediated at significant cost and effort, which includes careful application of water with proper drainage to carry away the accumulated salts.[25] With little excess water available, severely saline fields are usually abandoned rather than remediated.

Prospects for long-term expansion, or even continuation of current agriculture irrigation levels in the Tigris-Euphrates basin at current levels are not good, and without water management and irrigation reforms, any short-term increases in Turkish irrigation will only come at further cost to Iraqi and Syrian agricultural capacity and water quality. In addition to achieving equitable and accepted water sharing between the three countries, improving irrigation efficiency is critical to meeting future water demands for not only agricultural, but also domestic and industrial sectors. Technical and policy recommendations to improve irrigation efficiency and promote domestic conservation are discussed later in this paper as a "soft path" forward, versus the "hard path" of increased reservoir construction and impoundment, river diversion, and exploitation of limited groundwater aquifers.

Distrust and Failed Attempts toward Agreement

Mechanisms for discussing and negotiating regional water management in the Tigris-Euphrates basin existed in various forms since the end of World War II, but have been ineffective in facilitating a formal water-sharing agreement. Negotiations have resulted in limited Turkey-Syria and Syria-Iraq bilateral agreements, with no tripartite agreements that address equitable water allocation to balance the basin's water resources and needs. The only formal water agreement between Turkey and Iraq is the 1946 Treaty of Friendship and Good Neighbors, which provided an opportunity to study and discuss water management before there were any large dams in place. Under the treaty, Turkey agreed to monitor and share flow data of the two rivers with Iraq. Both countries agreed that control of the rivers depended largely on actions taken by Turkey in their headwaters, however the treaty also called for a separate consultation and agreement for each major Turkish work installed on the rivers.[26] As development of the Tigris and Euphrates rivers began in the mid-1960s, bilateral and tripartite meetings were held, occasionally with Soviet involvement, but with no formal agreements.[27] When the filling of Lake Assad behind Tabqa Dam cut Euphrates River flows into Iraq and nearly led to Iraqi-Syrian military conflict in 1975, Saudi Arabia mediated a June agreement where Syria agreed to pass 60 percent of the Euphrates River flow it received from Turkey through to Iraq.[28] With this agreement, Iraq and Syria remained relatively unified through the 1990s in their criticism of continued Turkish dam construction and irrigation project development. However the political upheaval and unrest in Syria have disrupted this relationship, with the Iraqi government distancing itself from the Assad regime, and Sunni groups in Iraq's Anbar province smuggling weapons to Syrian opposition fighters.[29]

In 1980 Turkey and Iraq established the Joint Technical Committee on Regional Waters to share data on planned projects and water utilization, and were joined by Syria in 1983. In 1984 Turkey submitted a Euphrates River water management plan to the committee, a requirement imposed by World Bank for continued funding for construction of the Ataturk Dam, although Syria and Iraq refused to sign the plan since it contained no commitments from Turkey on minimum water flows or allocations. In sixteen separate meetings, the Joint Technical Committee never made progress in reconciling the Turkish, Syrian, and Iraqi positions, including the purpose of the committee itself. While Syria and Iraq sought to use the committee for discussions of Euphrates water allocation, Turkey limited its participation to technical data exchange.[30] In the aftermath of spiking tensions during the filling of Lake Ataturk in 1990-1992, the committee disbanded in 1993.

Turkey has employed a strategy of using its control over the basin's water to its political advantage over Syria and Iraq. After Ataturk Dam construction began in 1983, Syria retaliated by increasing material and sanctuary support to Kurdish Workers Party (PKK) rebels, prompting Turkey to threaten a complete cutoff of the Euphrates flows into Syria. This situation led to a 1987 visit by Turkish President Turgut Ozal to Damascus, during which an agreement was signed guaranteeing a Euphrates River flow of 500 m³/s at the Turkish-Syrian border, while Syria promised to eject and cease support to the PKK.[31] While this agreed water volume was in accordance with prior

Syrian requests, it discounted the Iraqi position, since Iraq had insisted since 1967 that

it receive the same amount at the Syrian-Iraqi border.[32] In following years Turkey tacitly

linked water flows into Syria and Iraq with cooperation against PKK infiltrators,

prompting Iraq and Syria to complain to the Arab League in 1990 that Turkey's Ataturk

Dam gave it a weapon of war.[33] In 1992 President Ozal stated that Turkey would not

inflict damage to Iraq and Syria if they cooperated against the PKK, and Prime Minister

Demirel stated, "It is impossible to engage in negotiations over water while allowing

terrorism."[34] Turkey's translation of its strategic water position into political and

economic power over Syria and Iraq sets a dangerous precedent where access to a

basic human need is used to compel behavior of neighboring governments.

Predictions of pending Turkey-Syria-Iraq armed conflict over water were put on

hiatus by the 1991 Gulf War and 2003 invasion of Iraq by the United States. However

severe 2008-2010 droughts have magnified the effect of upstream water impoundment

and withdrawals. In 2009, Iraqi Prime Minister Al-Malaki and other Iraqi ministers

charged that Turkey and Syria were not keeping previous promises to maintain

Euphrates River flows, resulting in shortages of drinking water and the collapse of Iraqi

irrigated agriculture.[35] During severe summer droughts, Turkey did not maintain the

previously promised 500 m^3/s flow of the Euphrates River into Syria, and stated that it

did not have water to spare from its reservoirs. After vehement protests by the Iraq

government, Turkey agreed to increase flows to between 450-500m^3/second, but only

for one month, to support limited irrigation of fall crop planting in Syria and Iraq.[36] The

most promising recent development occurred in April 2008, when Turkey, Syria and Iraq agreed to establish a regional water institute to jointly study water needs and available resources. The institute will include 18 water experts from each country, while conducting its studies at the Ataturk Dam facilities.

<u>Access to Water, Right or a Resource?</u>

The fundamental issue that shapes viewpoints in water politics is how access to water is defined. There is no disputing that water is a fundamental human and societal need. However, is equitable access to water a fundamental and universal human right, and thus a responsibility for governments to provide to citizens, and to equitably share with cross-border neighbors? Or is water a resource commodity that can rightfully be controlled by individuals, corporations, or states that have privileged access through property ownership, national boundaries, topography, or geography? The United Nations and other international organizations have strongly affirmed the human right to sufficient and safe water, and have linked this right to developing international water law. However, other water development forums have stopped short of endorsing access to water as a human right, largely due to blocking actions by influential nations and sponsor groups.

The strongest official statement to date on the human right to water is the United Nations Economic and Social Council General Comment Number 15, passed in November 2002, which states the "human right to water" is "indispensable for leading a life in human dignity" and "a prerequisite for the realization of other human rights."[37] Human dignity and other human rights linked to water include "the highest attainable standard of health and the rights to adequate housing and adequate food."[38] General Comment 15 is part of the International Covenant on Economic, Social, and Cultural Rights, and calls on states to take steps to ensure sustainable and equitable access to clean water for their citizens, and to protect water supplies from pollution. The covenant also extends this obligation to international relationships, referencing the 1997 United Nations Convention on the Law of Non-navigational Uses of International Watercourses stating, "International cooperation requires States parties to refrain from actions that interfere, directly or indirectly, with the enjoyment of the right to water in other countries."[39] In the event of conflict between two or more states over a shared water resource, the covenant calls on each state to "prevent significant harm" and "consider the requirements of vital human needs of its neighbors."[40]

Other forums have fallen short of affirming access to water as a basic human right, including the 3rd International Water Forum held in Kyoto during March 2003. While the forum's Ministerial Declaration called water "indispensable for human health and welfare," it omits language specifically naming water access as a human right.[41] This omission led a coalition of water-focused NGOs to issue their own declaration from Kyoto that said, "water is a public good and access to safe, affordable water is a human right." The NGO statement chastised forum ministers to "reaffirm that access to water and sanitation is a basic human right in the Kyoto Declaration" and to "respect and protect human rights in all water policy and water resource management decisions."[42] Opposed to the forum's call for an increase in private financing for dam construction and large water infrastructure, the NGO statement cautioned that "Governments, International Financial Institutions, and the private sector should cease to promote water mega-projects without reference to international agreements and must always incorporate the recommendations of the World Commission on Dams into water and energy planning processes."[43] Water equity and conservation proponents blame the reluctance of influential governments and private corporations for the removal of human water rights from international conference agendas. The United States is singled out as an obstacle to wider discussion of water as a human right, since "for at least one of the major water conferences held in the past few years, they explicitly removed the phrase 'water is a human right' from the conference statement."[44] United States reluctance to endorse the right to water in a non-binding conference statement is questionable, but may be partially explained by not wanting to introduce new challenges into long-running water negotiations between Israel, Jordan, Lebanon, Syria, and the Palestinian West Bank over Jordan River and underground water resources.

Barriers to Agreement- Principles that Frame Interactions of Riparian States

The rise of early Mesopotamian civilizations occurred because central governments were able to harness water resources by constructing and maintaining complex canal systems that diverted Tigris and Euphrates rivers waters for large-scale irrigation. Control of the water for irrigation was the source of food and power, thus governments jealously protected and asserted power over waters within their borders.[45] This notion of water as a source of national power, or "water nationalism," is a strong cultural component that quickly polarizes Middle East water politics. The challenge of managing relationships between upstream-downstream riparians is inherently problematic, since these riparians begin with distinctly unequal access to river flows, and thus unequal levels of national power.

In upstream-downstream relationships, riparians will likely adhere to principles on opposing ends of a negotiating spectrum, which can be described as "absolute territorial sovereignty" for upstream riparian states, and "absolute territorial integrity" for downstream riparian states.[46] The principle of absolute territorial sovereignty allows that

13

a state has absolute authority to dispose of any waters that originate or flow through its territory, but also gives it no right to expect uninterrupted inward river flows from other states.[47] This principle is also referred to as the "Harmon Doctrine," after United States Attorney General Judson Harmon. Responding in 1895 to protests by the Mexican government over US withdrawals from the Rio Grande River, Harmon stated that, "the rules, precedents, and principles of international law impose no liability or obligation on the United States."[48] This principle of territorial sovereignty over waters or right of first use obviously favors the most upstream riparian in a shared basin, and is clearly reflected in the Turkish government assertion of sovereignty over all of the Tigris and Euphrates waters that rise within its borders. Echoing the Harmon Doctrine, Turkish President Suleiman Demiral stated in 1991, "Why should they [Syria and Iraq] have rights to the waters of Turkey? Do we have the right to the oil of these downstream countries? The upstream people have the absolute right to use this water. The Turkish waters are not international waters."[49]

The second principle of water relationships represents the opposite viewpoint, of absolute territorial integrity, where a state has a right to demand the natural flow of water into its territory, but also cannot restrict it from flowing into another country. This principle favors the lowest riparian nation, and reflects the interests of Iraq in the Tigris-Euphrates basin, Israel in the Jordan basin, and Egypt in the Nile basin. In 1981 Egyptian President Sadat warned that "If Ethiopia takes any action to block the Nile waters, there will be no alternative for us but to use force. Tampering with the rights of a nation to water is tampering with its life and a decision to go to war on this score is indisputable in the international community."[50] Neither of these first two principals will lead to agreement, since they represent unrealistic, individualistic and self-serving interests.

A third water agreement principle is a combination of the previous two, involving restricted water sovereignty and restricted territorial integrity, where nations in a regional drainage basin balance their national water interests with the water needs and national power of neighbors, based on a combination of relationships and bargaining over demands and concessions.[51] This principle is the default position of a mid-stream riparian such as Syria, however the principle still favors the upstream riparian, whose stronger position gives it negotiating advantage, and also little interest in reaching an agreement that limits its water use unless the downstream riparian provides significant concessions. In these situations, the involvement and influence of external states and organizations may be needed to induce cooperation between the riparians.

Relative military power obviously affects water politics between riparian nations sharing a river basin, and a militarily strong downstream riparian will likely threaten or use military force against an upstream riparian to maintain river flows into its country. Egypt and Israel have been able to offset their respective downstream positions on the Nile and Jordan rivers due to their superior military power and political clout relative to their upstream neighbors. Israel has compensated for its downstream position by seizing key terrain that increases its access to key water sources, including the Litani and Hashbani rivers in southern Lebanon, and the Golan Heights in Syria. Israel's water strategy has always included the resolve to take by force what it could not secure in negotiations. In contrast, the Tigris-Euphrates basin is greatly imbalanced, where Turkey's superior military power, augmented by its NATO membership and economic

15

relationship with Europe, solidifies its already overwhelming hydro-strategic position. Even if Iraq and Syria could ally themselves firmly against Turkey, their combination is no match against Turkish military power, and there are no feasible military objectives that could be seized or destroyed to significantly change the situation. The Ataturk Dam is far too large to destroy by airpower, and it is also heavily-protected by Turkish air defenses.[52] Iraq and Syria therefore have only a few diplomatic options to influence Turkey's water management policies, primarily by appealing to regional and international organizations in the context of Turkish international law violations, and by enlisting the support of other regional or international powers that can influence Turkey, primarily Saudi Arabia or the United States.

International Water Law and International Organizations

Most of the world's shared or trans-boundary waters are already regulated by watercourse-specific treaties, limited interstate agreements, or umbrella agreements covering regional waters. The notion of an international drainage basin, where the major rivers, tributaries, and groundwater shared by neighboring riparian states comprise an integrated system is well-established in international water law principles. The International Law Institute's 1911 Madrid Declaration, the International Law Association's 1967 Helsinki Rules, and the International Law Commission's draft articles for the UN Law of Non-Navigational Use of International Watercourses all recognized the integrated drainage basin as the necessary level of analysis and coverage for international law.[53] The deliberations and recommendations from these bodies provided useful general principles, but follow-on attempts to expand the scope and acceptance of international water law have resulted in weakened, passive compromise statements, with limited mechanisms for enforcement. As a result, international water law is still undeveloped and markedly weak compared to the challenges and risks of water competition in the contested basins of the Middle East.

Despite the thousands of existing water laws, agreements and treaties, the only universal treaty on freshwater is the 1997 United Nations Convention on the Non-Navigational Uses of International Watercourses, also known as the UN Water Convention.[54] Adoption of this treaty in May 1997 came nearly thirty years after the UN General Assembly asked the International Law Commission to prepare a set of rules for international watercourses. In preparing draft articles between 1987 and 1990, the commission's thirty-four international lawyers soon encountered significant opposition from downstream riparians to the term "drainage basin," along with "international watercourse system" and "shared natural resource."[55] When the Commission finally submitted draft articles for the law in 1994, it already contained significant compromises that weakened its scope and usefulness. The word "system" was enclosed in brackets throughout the document, indicating the commission had not reached a decision on its inclusion, and neither the words "shared," nor "shared natural resource" appeared anywhere.[56] It seemed as if the ILC had backed off from the integrated basin concept and the interdependence of its components, which was the keystone of the Helsinki Rules of 1967 published thirty years earlier by the International Law Association.

The 1997 UN Water Convention does convey key principles on the importance of consultation, cooperation, and equity between riparian states. Throughout the articles, the principle of "equitable and reasonable utilization" of international rivers is repeated, with Article 5 stating, "Countries should use water from international rivers in fair and reasonable ways."[57] Another significant principle is the obligation to not cause significant harm, with Article 7 stating that a watercourse state must "take all appropriate measures to prevent the causing of significant harm to other watercourse States." Article 7 further describes how a watercourse state that does cause significant harm to another must take appropriate measures to eliminate the harm and discuss compensation with the affected state.[58] The articles emphasize cooperation and negotiation, charging riparian states to work together on the use, development, and protection of river systems and their water. Although the principles of equity and reasonable use, obligation against causing harm, notification, and cooperation are certainly desired aspects of riparian state relationships, they are also restatements of customary law, and at best a framework for constructing more specific water management agreements. The phrase "equitable and reasonable utilization" is obviously vague enough to allow wide interpretation by upstream and downstream riparians, and is also heavily influenced by numerous factors unique to the situation in a particular drainage basin. The committee acknowledges this by listing seven "relevant factors and circumstances" in Article 6 of the Convention, including "social and economic needs of the countries involved" and "the effects of the use of rivers in one country on other countries."[59] The importance placed on negotiations in the document by default favors the interests of stronger riparian states, especially those such as Turkey, who can also negotiate from a superior upstream position. Overall, the political compromises made in seeking wider acceptance of the law have resulted in broad, elastic terms that provide limited practical guidance to mediating water-sharing issues between Turkey, Syria, and Iraq, and are at best a useful framework for a long, arduous process of seeking a long-term water-sharing agreement in the Tigris-Euphrates basin.

The United Nations General Assembly approved the Convention on International Watercourses by a large majority on May 21, 1997 with 103 states voting for approval, while three states, Turkey, China, and Burundi, voted against adoption.[60] For it to enter into force, thirty-five member states must officially become parties to the convention, and as of January 2009, seventeen states had either ratified, accepted, approved, or acceded to the convention.[61] The split between stronger and weaker riparian states is reflected in the parties to the convention. Syria, Iraq, Jordan, and Lebanon have all become parties, while Turkey, Israel, and Egypt have not. Turkey explained its opposition vote to the convention by stating it would provide Syria and Iraq with de facto veto power over Turkish upstream development. Furthermore, the Turkish ambassador insisted that the convention failed to mention "the indisputable principle of the sovereignty of the watercourse states over the parts of international watercourses situated in their territory."[62] This adherence by Turkey to the principle of absolute territorial sovereignty over the waters of the Tigris and Euphrates flowing within its borders is essentially a rejection that they are international watercourses at all, and not subject to regulation by international law. Turkey's position in this 1997 General Assembly vote is ironic, since the convention contains similar language with the water management plan it submitted to the Joint Technical Committee in 1984 for the Ataturk Dam and reservoir, which called for "optimal, equitable and reasonable utilization of the transboundary watercourses of the Euphrates-Tigris basin."[63]

The World Bank and World Commission on Dams

As the first and primary financier of large dam projects in developing countries, the World Bank is both praised for promoting economic development, and heavily criticized for contributing to social upheaval, environmental degradation, and regional water competition. The Bank has been accused of facilitating national and macroeconomic benefits at the expense of displaced local or indigenous communities, downstream riparians, and vulnerable ecosystems. The Bank has long considered the protests of downstream riparian states when rewiewing funding requests for large dam projects, and as early as the 1970s Syria attempted to delay Turkish GAP progress by objecting to construction of the Karakaya Dam on the Euphrates River. However, since the Karakaya was primarily a hydro-power project and would not significantly reduce the river's flow, the World Bank provided 70 percent of the dam's funding over Syria's protest.[64] Syria and Iraq both protested when Turkey sought World Bank funding for the Ataturk Dam, and since the massive irrigation works associated with the dam would clearly reduce the Euphrates flows, the Bank required that Turkey submit a water management plan for Syrian and Iraqi approval. When Syria and Iraq rejected Turkey's plan submission to the Joint Technical Committee in 1984, Turkey was forced to proceed without World Bank loans by raising internal funds and awarding construction contracts to Turkish companies.[65] This effort delayed, but did not prevent construction of the Ataturk Dam, and made the dam an even greater symbol of Turkish nationalism.

Influenced by international controversy surrounding the Ataturk Dam and other large dam projects worldwide, the World Bank and International Union for Conservation of Nature and Natural Resources (IUCN) in 1997 jointly proposed that a World Commission on Dams study the economic, social, and environmental impacts of the development of large dam projects. Established in 1998, the 12-member commission reviewed the effectiveness of large dams, assessed alternatives for water and energy development, and developed internationally acceptable standards for the planning, design, construction, and operation of dams.[66] The Report of the World Commission on Dams, published in 2000, criticizes Turkey as a "regional power that holds an upstream position," enabling it to "implement projects without consultation."[67] The report calls for a rethinking of decision-making on dams, and emphasizes involvement of affected stakeholders throughout the assessment and planning process, particularly stakeholders who will require resettlement and compensation. The report's impact on progress of the GAP's highly-controversial Ilisu Dam was dramatic. Although the project was not funded by the World Bank, the Turkish government's failure to address many of the report's guidelines and criteria caused private German, Swiss, and Austrian lenders to withdraw $610 million in export-credit project funding in 2008.   Syrian and Iraqi protests, along with pressure from international organizations and lenders, have slowed Turkey's GAP progress, but they are unable to halt or compel changes to dam projects as long as Turkey can raise internal funding. As with the Ataturk Dam, Turkish leaders have pledged to continue construction of the Ilisu Dam, although completion has been delayed until at least 2015.[68]

The Colorado River Compact and United States-Mexico Water Treaty

Since the current state of international water law provides at best a framework for more specific water agreements between basin states, it is useful to look comparatively at the history of water agreements in other arid river basins, and the Colorado River basin in particular. The water resources of the Colorado River basin have been among the most contested in the western hemisphere, both within the United States and between the United States and Mexico. Water-sharing and management of the basin is now structured around two different agreements, the 1922 Colorado River Compact and the 1944 United States-Mexico Water Treaty. While these agreements don't fully represent the highest ideals of international water law, they include balance between upstream-downstream interests, equity and respect among states, flexibility combined with downstream flow guarantees, effective joint implementation and oversight, and recourse to submit disagreements to higher legal authority.

The first implemented agreement was the Colorado River Compact, which was negotiated between seven states of the southwestern United States and signed in 1922. When planned dam-building by California in the 1920s signaled a looming race over storage and diversion of Colorado River water, the basin states voluntarily began negotiations to pre-empt more invasive U.S. federal involvement and costly state-to-state litigation.[69] After attempts to negotiate individual water allocations for each state, representatives found it was less contentious to divide the negotiations between the Upper Basin states of Colorado, New Mexico, Utah, and Wyoming, and the Lower Basin states of Arizona, California, and Nevada.[70] The resulting Colorado River Compact of 1922 balanced the upstream and downstream interests by initially allocating 7.5 million acre-feet of withdrawals annually to each basin, but recognized the greater growth potential in the populous southern states by adding an additional 1 million acre-feet annually to the Lower Basin allocation. The states of each entity were then free to negotiate the division of each basin's annual allocation. While the Lower Basin states divided their allocation by water volumes, the Upper Basin states established fixed percentages of the total, which proved to be more advantageous to managing allocations during drought years.[71] To protect the Lower Basin states' allocation from preemptive withdrawals by the Upper Basin, the compact required a minimum ten-year average river flow of 75 million acre-feet at the boundary between the basins.

The Colorado River Compact has been supplemented by upper and lower basin agreements, federal laws, regulatory agreements, and U.S. federal court decisions. For contentious issues that could not be remedied through lateral negotiations between states, the United States federal courts system has provided a backstop for binding decisions to preserve the compact. In 1952 Arizona filed suit against California in the United States Supreme Court in a Lower Basin dispute, and although the case was not concluded for eleven years, it provided a definitive water allocation between the Lower Basin states that endures today.[72] From its beginning, the compact recognized the primacy of the federal government by including provisions for a future international water agreement, reserving all excess river flows beyond the Upper and Lower Basin withdrawals for allocation to Mexico in a future treaty with the United States. If that amount proved insufficient to meet requirements of a future treaty, the Upper and Lower basin would equally divide and bear the deficit.[73]

Progress toward a water treaty with Mexico began in 1924 when the United States Congress authorized the President to name three commissioners to study the equitable division of Rio Grande River waters with Mexico, and in 1927 the commissioners were further authorized to link the waters of both the Colorado and Rio Grande rivers in negotiations.[74] However it was not until 1944 that the United States-Mexico Water Treaty was finally completed and signed. This treaty marked a tremendous shift from the Harmon Doctrine, and the United States, as the Colorado River's upstream riparian, now guaranteed Mexico 1.5 million acre-feet of Colorado River water annually, 9 percent of the river's average annual flow, despite the growing pressure of irrigation and domestic development on the American side. Balancing

United States interests was a guarantee from the Mexican Government to provide an average of 350,000 acre-feet annually to the United States from tributaries of the Rio Grande River for irrigation use by Texas farmers.[75] Thus the treaty balanced each nation's desire for water in two separate basins, a trade made possible by each country's respective upstream position on the two rivers.

What has proven one of the treaty's key provisions is the formation of the International Boundary Waters Commission (IBWC), a joint organization consisting of American and Mexican commissioners, proven invaluable in implementing the terms of the treaty through technical monitoring, flow scheduling, documentation, and dispute resolution. The IBWC matches up Mexico's requested water delivery schedule with monitored deliveries by the United States, jointly operates gauging stations along the rivers, and resolves routine disputes through a series of decisions adopted as "minutes," which are binding.[76] Records of the rivers' flows are published annually in IBWC bulletins, in both English and Spanish. The effectiveness and empowerment of the IBWC provides the United States-Mexico treaty with valuable flexibility and adaptability for implementation, and serves as an organizational model for promoting cooperation between Middle East basin states.

The United States-Mexico treaty has survived various larger disputes between the two countries, including a 1961 environmental complaint by Mexico that the United States was violating the treaty and international law by sending highly-saline discharges from irrigation projects into the river. In a 1972 agreement, the United States agreed to maintain the environmental quality of the river entering Mexico at the same level of quantity as water withdrawn in the United States. At United States' expense, a bypass

24

channel was constructed to divert the saline waters directly to the Gulf of California, followed by construction of a desalination plant to process the agricultural runoff, allowing it to be returned to the river.[77] Other treaty enforcement mechanisms have evolved through economic cooperation, and in 2004 Texas irrigation districts and farmers filed suit under the 1994 North American Free Trade Agreement (NAFTA) over non-delivery of water by Mexico into the Rio Grande.[78]

The relationships between American states in negotiating the Colorado River compact, the tradeoffs and structure of the United States-Mexico water treaty, and more importantly the evolution of that treaty since 1944 are instructive to international water law and politics today. Considering how the alignment of interests between the states of the Upper and Lower Colorado River basin contributed to the Colorado River compact, Iraq and Syria would be well-served to keep their interests and positions closely aligned in any water negotiations with Turkey. The inclusion of both the Colorado and Rio Grande rivers in negotiations between the United States and Mexico allowed for tradeoffs that can be a model for Turkish-Syrian-Iraqi discussions by linking negotiations on both the Tigris and Euphrates rivers. As the United States demonstrated progression from the "Harmon Doctrine" toward a more equitable water relationship with Mexico, so should Turkey feel compelled to limit its water withdrawals and development to preserve the critical water supplies for Iraq and Syria. Finally, all three countries should continue to develop a system for technical cooperation and coordination, creating an organization similar to the United States-Mexico International Boundary and Water Commission to implement an eventual water-sharing treaty.

The Proposed United States Role and Options

On 15 December 2011, the day Multinational Force-Iraq command cased its colors in Baghdad, President Obama stopped short of calling the nine-year U.S. involvement in Iraq a victory, but did say that U.S. troops had given "the Iraqis their country in a way that gives them a chance for a successful future."[79] The United States' ten-year investment in building security, civil capacity, and democratic governance in Iraq may be wasted if Iraq's economic future and stability are consistently threatened by water crisis, and regional security is decreased by the potential for water conflict. The U.S. has the ability to influence both Turkey and Iraq towards a long-term water management agreement; however the current instability in Syria and the international isolation of the Assad regime will likely preclude trilateral negotiations involving Syria. If Syrian regime change occurs, assistance in shaping long-term water sharing negotiations could be a foundation for building productive relationships with a new government, and U.S. influence in negotiations could be held as an incentive for near-term Syrian political reforms. Overall, a long-term water sharing agreement between Turkey, Syria, and Iraq could lead to expanded cooperation and relationships between these countries, which could produce a bloc friendly to United States interests, able to limit Iranian regional influence.

The United States role in promoting water negotiations between Turkey, Syria, and Iraq could involve a range of options, including supporting trilateral negotiations from the background, facilitating resolution through the United Nations, or directly brokering talks with U.S.-led mediation. Supporting negotiations from the background continues current United States policy which regards the issue of Tigris-Euphrates River basin water management as a regional affair. Even in a behind-the-scenes role, the

26

U.S. must be prepared to provide both positive and negative incentives to Turkey and Iraq to facilitate an agreement, such as increased Foreign Military Funding (FMF) and Foreign Military Sales (FMS), trade agreements, financial assistance to improve water infrastructure, or technical assistance to improve agriculture irrigation techniques. This option promotes expansion of Turkish and Iraqi bilateral diplomacy, but has a relatively low chance of producing an agreement that actually safeguards Iraqi water supplies, since Turkey has little incentive to cede its dominant control over the region's water resources and sacrifice future development in the Southeast Anatolia region. The risk of this option is that no effective agreement is reached, and critical seasonal Iraqi water shortages continue. As a modification to this option, the U.S. could request that a regional organization, such as the Arab League, broker the trilateral negotiations to increase influence on the parties.

If the U.S. takes an expanded role in shepherding this issue to the United Nations, there are potential benefits and risks to U.S. interests in the Jordan and Nile river basins, and even for U.S. relations with Mexico over the Colorado and Rio Grande rivers. The U.S. Ambassador to the United Nations and the U.S. Secretary of State can facilitate Iraq's effort to bring the dispute over Tigris-Euphrates River use to the Security Council and the International Court of Justice. U.S. support for the Iraqi position that the rivers are both subject to the United Nations Water Convention, and a request for mediation of Turkey-Syria-Iraq negotiations could strengthen the credibility and provide precedent to international water law. However, this policy action would logically require that the U.S. first accept and become party to the United Nations Water Convention, which the U.S. has thus far declined to do, despite voting for it in 1997. However U.S.

27

acceptance and possible ratification of the convention could also strengthen Lebanese, Syrian, and Jordanian claims against Israel regarding Jordan River valley waters. Even with United Nations-brokered negotiations, the U.S. must still be prepared to provide military and economic aid incentives to facilitate Turkish concessions and guarantees in the agreement. In exchange for the diplomatic support, the U.S. should pressure Iraq to take definitive steps to promote Sunni and Kurd representation in Iraqi government ministries and parliament, significantly curb Iranian influence in the country's political process, and halt open Iranian intelligence-gathering from Iraq's security forces. This option's risk includes rejection of the Iraqi position by the Security Council, where China may block support due to its own water-sharing issues with its neighbors in Southeast Asia.[80] Even if the International Law Commission recognizes Iraq's claim that the Tigris and Euphrates rivers are international watercourses, Turkey may not recognize the decision and refuse to participate in United Nations-mediated negotiations without significant additional U.S. and NATO influence.

Direct U.S. mediation of water-sharing talks between Turkey, Syria, and Iraq, outside of a United Nations framework, still provides the U.S. opportunity to gain and exert influence and promote long-term stability, while avoiding the difficulties of seeking United Nations involvement and the disagreements over international water law interpretation. The U.S. should expect to expend significant diplomatic effort to gain Turkish concessions, to restrict future Turkish exploitation of Tigris and Euphrates flows in order to preserve Syrian, but primarily Iraqi access to surface water. The same economic and military incentives are available, and the U.S. should issue the same demands to Iraq as described previously in exchange for mediation. With U.S. prestige on the line, risks include Turkish stonewalling and demands for greater aid incentives than the U.S. is prepared to provide. Turkey will likely demand Iraqi and Syrian cooperation in Kurdish pacification and anti-PKK operations that could destabilize the current delicate balance between Iraq's central government and the Kurdish autonomous region. However this option is most likely to produce agreement in the least time, and the U.S. has the opportunity to secure maximum leverage with Iraq against Iranian influence.

In all options, a combination of incentives will likely be needed to induce Turkey to make water management concessions that could cost it hydroelectric generation capacity and future agricultural production in Southeast Anatolia. Positive incentives include increased aid to Turkey in the form Foreign Military Funding (FMF), International Military Education and Training (IMET) funds, or State Department economic support funds. Since Turkey is a NATO member and a close regional U.S. ally, use of negative incentives should be limited to diplomatic pressure, including public calls for Turkish cooperation and concessions on water-sharing. Effective implementation of a water-sharing treat will require verification of flows in and out of Turkish reservoirs, at national boundaries, and water withdrawals by all three countries. The United States can play a role here also by advising on the implementation of an organization similar to the IWBC, and by assisting with installation of jointly-monitored water level and flow gauges at key river structures and points, which would provide real-time water data to all three countries.

Alternative Water Strategies for Syria and Iraq

For Syria and Iraq to continue to grow their populations and economies with shrinking water supplies, alternative water strategies must be implemented that make the most of available water resources. These alternative strategies must include the managed diversification of water sources and deliberate water conservation in agricultural, industrial, and domestic sectors. Through careful management of their limited groundwater supplies, both Syria and Iraq can reduce their reliance on surface water from the Tigris and Euphrates rivers, and for Iraq, desalination of sea water is an additional, but daunting option. However, the greatest opportunity for improved water security lies in conservation, and since 80 percent or more of regional water withdrawals are for irrigation, even a modest reform in agricultural irrigation practices can produce a dramatic effect. Irrigation reforms could range from simple improvements such as better canal maintenance and scheduling to deliver water to fields only when it is actually needed, to conversion from flood or furrow irrigation to sprinkler and drip-tube systems. However, implementation of these strategies requires funding, administration and oversight, compliance enforcement, and most importantly, the education and cooperation of citizens and stakeholders.

With surface water from the Tigris and Euphrates rivers supplying only about half of the land area of Iraq and Syria, the primarily rural population in the remaining areas are reliant on groundwater wells.[81] According to Aquastat, the United Nations Food and Agriculture Organization information system on water and agriculture, groundwater resources for both Iraq and Syria are extremely limited, totaling 3.2 km^3 and 4.8km^3 of renewable water annually for each country respectively.[82] Unfortunately much of this groundwater is brackish to saline, and contains high concentrations of other minerals, including carbonates, sulphates, and chlorides, which make the water extremely "hard." These minerals scale in pipes and boilers, and when consumed can cause diarrhea and

30

stone formation within the body.[83] As a result, most of Iraq's groundwater requires treatment to remove suspended solids and minerals, and in some cases requires desalination before it meets world health standards for domestic consumption.

The limitations of Syria's and Iraq's aquifers also require careful management and efficient use, if groundwater is to serve as a partial and sustainable replacement for surface water, particularly for small-scale irrigation projects. However, uncontrolled digging of wells and groundwater pumping has proliferated, especially since 2003 in Iraq, while the government lacked authority, guidelines, and resources for oversight of these activities. As a result, aquifer levels and water quality have dropped significantly, particularly in the ancient "karez" underground aqueducts in Iraqi Kurdistan.[84] Unless Iraq's Ministry of Water, along with Kurdish authorities and local officials, establish and enforce controls on well-digging and groundwater pumping, Iraq's valuable but limited aquifers will be depleted within a few years. Syria faces similar problems, where overuse has dropped groundwater levels precipitously, forcing farmers to either install deeper and larger pumps or leave their lands, while putting water supplies for major cities including Damascus at risk.[85] In both countries, the groundwater supplies are overextended, with significant wastage occurring from leaky infrastructure and inefficient irrigation.

Desalination- Holy Grail of Water Supply or Last Resort?

With 97% of the globe's water contained in its oceans and seas, desalination of ocean water or saline groundwater has long been considered the "holy grail" of freshwater supply, a cost-effective solution for water-short regions.[86] Improved technology and experience in plant construction and operation are beginning to lower desalination costs, and as water demand continues to rise, large-scale desalination projects are in various stages of planning or construction throughout the world. Countering desalination's potential benefits are significant capital, technical, and environmental challenges of plant construction, and high operating and maintenance costs. In most regions there are still other alternatives to desalination such as freshwater imports via pipeline or off-setting conservation efforts, like reduced agricultural irrigation, that can be achieved at lower cost.[87] However, in regions where there are few water supply options, and water conservation has already been employed, desalination is an increasingly popular option. As Iraq's population grows and water supply decreases, large-scale desalination will almost certainly be a necessary part of Iraq's water supply future, but it will have to overcome significant obstacles and may not meet expectations. Iraq's water planners should carefully consider the technologies, trends, opportunities, and challenges of desalination before committing hundreds of millions of dollars to plant construction.

Seawater desalination provides two extremely attractive benefits, a source of freshwater that is both relatively "drought-proof" and locally controlled.[88] Iraq's situation certainly justifies pursuit of a large-scale desalination capability on its Persian Gulf coast, but it is uncertain whether Iraq can successfully overcome the financial and technical obstacles of constructing and operating such a plant. Financial challenges are the most significant obstacle, and the required capital for plant and infrastructure construction is immense. A recent case in Tampa Bay, Florida is instructive, where construction of a 95,000 m^3/day reverse-osmosis (RO) plant budgeted for $110 million finally began operating at reduced capacity in late 2007, more than five years behind schedule and $48 million over budget.[89] After surviving the capital costs and difficulties of construction, a desalination plant still faces high operating costs. Energy is the biggest variable cost, and averages from 44 percent of operating costs for RO plants to 59 percent for multi-stage flash (MSF) distillation plants.[90] Saudi Arabia's 28 MSF plants provide 70% of the kingdom's drinking water, but also consume 1.5 million barrels of oil each day![91] In addition, desalination plants require expensive maintenance to replace stainless steel pumps, piping, electrical gear, and membranes. As a result, desalinated water is usually much more expensive than other freshwater, with worldwide costs ranging from approximately $0.70/m^3$ to $1.83/m^3$ of freshwater produced, however once costs of delivering the water to users is added, the cost rises to approximately $1/m^3$ to $3/m^3$.[92] This cost is two to three times higher than currently paid by most U.S. urban users. From a financial standpoint, the "holy grail" of water supply looks more like a last resort. There are ways to mitigate costs, including co-locating desalination activities with existing power plants to lower infrastructure costs for power lines and intake/discharge pipelines, however the initial costs for construction of large-scale desalination capability is still beyond the means of most countries.

Desalination is thus an available, but daunting option for supplementing Iraq's drinking and industrial water needs. Iraq is pursuing desalination of Persian Gulf water to partially supply municipal and industrial needs around Basra.[93] Iraq has also purchased 350 solar-powered desalination units, at a cost of $41 million, to purify brackish groundwater for rural villages.[94] However these and other desalination projects in Iraq have been funded primarily international donors, with equipment provided by foreign companies. These projects may not prove long-term financially or technically supportable by Iraq's struggling national ministries and local governments. Meeting the challenges of sighting, financing, constructing, committing the required energy resources, and operating large-scale desalination plants is likely beyond Iraq's current financial capability and technical expertise. Over the next decade desalination will provide at best a limited augmentation of Iraq's current freshwater resources, mostly through small-scale desalination of brackish groundwater for groups of rural villages. With these limitations, the Iraqi government and people would be better served by putting financial resources and efforts into water conservation.

Water Use Reform- An Imperative for Iraq's Future

Regardless of the policy option pursued by the U.S. government, and whether or not a long-term Tigris-Euphrates basin water-sharing agreement is reached, Syria, Iraq, and even Turkey must prepare for an increasingly dry future by looking inward and finding ways to use water more efficiently. This requires prioritizing irrigation reform, domestic conservation, and wastewater re-use ahead of conventional projects to increase water supplies. Peter Gleick, a world-renowned water reform expert, calls this re-thinking of water supply management the "soft path" of decreasing demand, versus the "hard path" of increasing supply through more dams, reservoirs, canals, pipelines and even desalination plants.[95] As the basin's upstream riparian, Turkey can continue to leverage "hard" options with more GAP dam construction, however additional water supply gains will come only at the expense of Syria and Iraq, further exacerbating tensions. Turkey's upstream actions leave Iraq and Syria with few conventional solutions for increasing water supplies, so they will be forced earlier toward water conservation reforms. With the bulk of their water use going to agriculture, irrigation reform will provide the greatest benefits, however domestic conservation, and wastewater reuse are also priorities, and all must be accomplished while regulating discharged waters to protect river environmental quality for downstream users.

Already driven by the combined effects of drought and upstream withdrawals, Iraqi farmers are slowly changing irrigation practices and equipment with government and NGO assistance. Sprinkler and drip-tube irrigation systems use less water than flooding or furrow irrigation techniques, especially when water is delivered to crops only when needed. Low-flow drip tube systems in particular can be supplied through groundwater, enabling irrigation of salt-resistant vegetable crops with brackish water supplies. By using less water, most soil salinity issues are reduced, since less salt is transported in with the irrigation water, and without water-logging, salt is not leached upward from the water table. Sprinkler and drip irrigation does not require installation and maintenance of expensive drainage systems to remove excess water and built-up salt encountered during flood irrigation. With saline return flows eliminated, rivers are less polluted from salt and fertilizer runoff, preserving downstream water quality.

Drawbacks of low-flow irrigation include equipment installation expenses and maintenance requirements, particularly for sprinkler systems. Drip systems are less expensive, but in 2003 the cost was an estimated at $1200-$2500 per hectare, beyond affordability for most small-scale farmers.[96] Farmers must also be trained on the equipment and irrigation techniques, but most importantly, they must learn to grow new crops. Low-flow irrigation is most suitable for row and tree crops, including vegetables, fruits, nuts, and dates, while unsuited to most cereal crops such as wheat, rice, and barley. Experts such as Gleick refer to this as "crop shifting" from low-value to high-value crops, but even with assistance, farmers' adjustment will depend on cultural influence, and ultimately on market prices.[97] The World Bank Group recently pledged to increase agricultural assistance to $6 billion to $8 billion per year, and the Bank is also the trustee of the Global Agriculture and Food Security Program (GAFSP), which funds long-term solutions to recurring food crises.[98] Since contributing donor countries are board members and can select which developing country applicant sits with them at meetings, the U.S. can assist Iraq's application to fund irrigation conversion.[99] Even assuming available funding for irrigation conversion, the toughest obstacle may be convincing Iraqi farmers, government ministries and the Iraqi public, who consider water from the Tigris and Euphrates rivers as a fundamental part of their national identity, to make efficiency and conservation a new priority.

Conclusion

This paper has attempted to describe the complex challenges of the Tigris and Euphrates river basin, which rival those of any disputed water basin in the Middle East and world in general. While near-term military conflict between Turkey, Syria, or Iraq over water is unlikely, persistent water shortages and inequities will contribute to human suffering, dislocation of rural populations, and economic hardships, challenging U.S. interests of regional governmental and economic stability. In Iraq, the worsening water situation will aggravate Sunni-Kurd-Shia ethnic conflicts, further challenging tenuous government stability and economic growth. As Syrian upheaval and conflict worsens, water shortages could contribute to a humanitarian crisis in that country. Turkey should restrain from taking advantage of Iraq's relative weakness and Syria's upheaval to continue its GAP development without consultation and consideration for downstream impacts. With vastly different upstream-downstream riparian viewpoints and interests, Turkey, Syria, and Iraq will not be able to resolve water allocation issues on their own,

36

as evidenced by nearly forty years of disagreement. The current state of international water law, to include the United Nations Water Convention, is too weak to force cooperation and concessions from the three countries. A long-term treaty for water sharing between Turkey, Syria, and Iraq is needed, and the United States should facilitate progress on a treaty through diplomacy and economic incentives, using lessons and models from the Colorado River Compact and U.S.-Mexico treaty. Finally, all three countries should make equitable efforts to use less water, emphasizing agricultural irrigation reform. In Syria and Iraq, international assistance will be particularly necessary to update irrigation infrastructure and assist farmers with shifts to more sustainable crops. Fortunately, despite the criticality of emerging water issues in Tigris and Euphrates river basin, conflicts have been avoided. However, these water issues will not become a catalyst for cooperation without the involvement of international and regional organizations, and the influence of the United States.

Endnotes

[1] Secretary-General Ban Ki-moon, "Address as prepared for delivery to the Davos World Economic Forum," UN News Centre, January 24, 2008, http://www.un.org/apps/news/infocus/sgspeeches/search_full.asp?statID=177 (accessed March 10, 2012).

[2] Aaron T. Wolf, "A Hydropolitical History of the Nile, Jordan and Euphrates River Basins," in Asit K. Biswas, *International Waters of the Middle East: From Euphrates-Tigris to Nile* (Oxford University Press, 1994), 26.

[3] Peter H. Gleick, "Water Conflict Chronology," in *The World's Water, 2008-2009: The Biennial Report on Freshwater Resources* (Washington, DC: Island Press, 2009), 167, 170.

[4] Sandra Postel, *The Last Oasis: Facing Water Scarcity* (New York: W.W. Norton and Co., 1992), 74.

[5] Analysis of Syria's ongoing internal upheaval is beyond the scope of this paper, but that upheaval and the potential fall of the Assad government will certainly weaken Syria's ability to pressure Turkey on water issues for some time.

[6]Masahiro Murakami, *Managing Water for Peace in the Middle East: Alternative Strategies* (Tokyo: United Nations University Press, 1995), 35.

[7]Ibid, 37.

[8]United Nations Food and Agriculture Organization, "Aquastat Country fact sheets for Turkey, Syria, and Iraq," December 9, 2011, http://www.fao.org/nr/water/aquastat/data/factsheets/aquastat_fact_sheet_tur_en.pdf, http://www.fao.org/nr/water/aquastat/data/factsheets/aquastat_fact_sheet_syr_en.pdf, http://www.fao.org/nr/water/aquastat/data/factsheets/aquastat_fact_sheet_irq_en.pdf (accessed 22 Jan 2012).

[9]Murakami, *Managing Water for Peace*, 36, 39.

[10]United States Central Intelligence Agency, *The World Factbook*, Country fact sheets for Turkey, Syria, and Iraq, January 4, 2012, https://www.cia.gov/library/publications/the-world-factbook/geos/tu.html, https://www.cia.gov/library/publications/the-world-factbook/geos/sy.html, https://www.cia.gov/library/publications/the-world-factbook/geos/iz.html (accessed January 15, 2012).

[11]United Nations Food and Agriculture Organization, "Country water briefs for Turkey, Syria, and Iraq," January 19, 2012, http://www.fao.org/nr/water/aquastat/data/wbsheets/aquastat_water_balance_sheet_tur_en.pdf, http://www.fao.org/nr/water/aquastat/data/wbsheets/aquastat_water_balance_sheet_syr_en.pdf, http://www.fao.org/nr/water/aquastat/data/wbsheets/aquastat_water_balance_sheet_irq_en.pdf (accessed January 19, 2012).

[12]Timothy Spence, "Cooperation Strategic to Protect Tigris and Euphrates," March 15, 2011, http://www.globalissues.org/news/2011/03/15/8895 (accessed January 17, 2012).

[13]Republic of Turkey, "GAP official website (English)", http://web.archive.org/web/20070222163710/http://www.gap.gov.tr/Flash/Ing/gaphrt/gharita/ggn4.jpg (accessed January 17, 2012).

[14]United States Department of Agriculture, Foreign Agriculture Service online, "GAP's Irrigation Component," http://www.fas.usda.gov/remote/mideast_pecad/turkey/turkey.htm (accessed January 17, 2012).

[15]United States Department of Agriculture, Foreign Agriculture Service, "Cotton World Markets and Trade" December 2007, http://usda01.library.cornell.edu/usda/fas/cotton-market//2000s/2007/cotton-market-12-01-2007.pdf (accessed January 17, 2012).

[16]Murakami, *Managing Water for Peace*, 42.

[17]United Nations Food and Agriculture Organization, "Syrian Arab Republic country profile," version 2008, http://www.fao.org/nr/water/aquastat/countries_regions/syria/index.stm (accessed January 17, 2012).

[18]Wolf, "A Hydropolitical History of the Nile, Jordan, and Euphrates River Basins", 29.

[19]CounterCurrent, "Dam Construction in Turkey and its Impact on Economic, Cultural, and Social Rights," March 14, 2011, http://m-h-s.org/ilisu/upload/PDF/2011/CESCR_Parallel_report_by_CounterCurrent_on_Turkish_dams_2011-03-14_f.pdf (accessed January 17, 2012).

[20]Juha I. Uitto and Jutta Schneider, eds., *Freshwater Resources in Arid Lands: UNU Global Environmental Forum V* (United Nations University Press: Tokyo, 1997), 90.

[21]United Nations Food and Agriculture Organization, "Fisheries and Aquaculture Department: Salinization of Waters," Updated 27 May 2005, http://www.fao.org/fishery/topic/13473/en (accessed February 10, 2012).

[22]United Nations Food and Agriculture Organization, "Aquastat Country fact sheets for Turkey, Syria, and Iraq," December 9, 2011, http://www.fao.org/nr/water/aquastat/data/factsheets/aquastat_fact_sheet_tur_en.pdf, http://www.fao.org/nr/water/aquastat/data/factsheets/aquastat_fact_sheet_syr_en.pdf, http://www.fao.org/nr/water/aquastat/data/factsheets/aquastat_fact_sheet_irq_en.pdf (accessed 22 Jan 2012).

[23]G. Abdelgawad, "Soil salinity monitoring and assessment in irrigated Arab agriculture," in *World Soil Resources Report Number 104*, 2009, http://www.fao.org/docrep/012/i1220e/i1220e.pdf (accessed January 30, 2012), 16.

[24]Karen Frenken, ed., *Irrigation in the Middle East region in figures: AQUASTAT Survey-2008* (Food and Agriculture Organization of the United Nations: Rome, 2009), 211.

[25]United Nations Food and Agriculture Organization, Agriculture and Consumer Protection Department, "Improving Irrigation Technology," March 2003, http://www.fao.org/ag/magazine/0303sp3.htm (accessed January 31, 2012).

[26]Greg Shapland, *Rivers of Discord* (St. Martin's Press, New York, 1997), 116.

[27]Wolf, "A Hydropolitical History of the Nile, Jordan, and Euphrates River Basins," 29.

[28]Ibid.

[29]The New York Times, "For Iraqis, Aid to Rebels in Syria Repays a Debt," February 12, 2012, http://www.nytimes.com/2012/02/13/world/middleeast/for-iraqis-aid-to-syrian-rebels-repays-a-war-debt.html?pagewanted=all (accessed March 3, 2012).

[30]Shapland, *Rivers of Discord*, 118.

[31]Joost Jongerden, "Dams and Politics in Turkey: Utilizing Water, Developing Conflict," *Middle East Policy Council* 17, no.1 (Spring 2010): 139.

[32]Wolf, "Hydropolitical History of the Nile, Jordan, and Euphrates River Basins," 35.

[33]Peter H. Gleick, "Water Conflict Chronology," in *The World's Water, 2004-2005: The Biennial Report on Freshwater Resources* (Washington, DC: Island Press, 2004), 245.

[34]Jongerden, "Dams and Politics in Turkey," 139.

[35]United Press International, "Water-short Iraq faces new peril: the sea," September 23, 2009, http://www.upi.com/Business_News/Energy-Resources/2009/09/23/Water-short-Iraq-faces-new-peril-the-sea/UPI-18861253720630/ (accessed February 24, 2012).

[36]Ecoworld Media, "Iraq's Water Crisis gets Worse Daily," September 23, 2009, http://www.ecoworld.com/energy-fuels/hydroelectric/water-short-iraq-faces-new-peril-sea.html (accessed February 10, 2012).

[37]Peter H. Gleick, "The Human Right to Water: Two Steps Forward, One Step Back," in *The World's Water, 2004-2005: The Biennial Report on Freshwater Resources* (Washington, DC: Island Press, 2004), 204.

[38]UN Committee on Economic, Social and Cultural Rights (CESCR), *General Comment No. 15: The Right to Water (Arts. 11 and 12 of the Covenant)*, January 20, 2003, http://www.unhcr.org/refworld/docid/4538838d11.html (accessed February 28, 2012), 1.

[39]Ibid, 11.

[40] Ibid.

[41]Nicholas Cain, "3rd World Water Forum in Kyoto: Disappointment and Possibility," in *The World's Water, 2004-2005: The Biennial Report on Freshwater Resources* (Washington, DC: Island Press, 2004), 192.

[42]Peter H. Gleick, "NGO Statement of the 3rd World Water Forum," in *The World's Water, 2004-2005: The Biennial Report on Freshwater Resources* (Washington, DC: Island Press, 2004), 202.

[43]Ibid.

[44]Gleick, "The Human Right to Water: Two Steps Forward, One Step Back," 205.

[45]Gwyn Rowley, "Political Controls of River Waters and Abstractions between Various States within the Middle East," in Hussein A. Amery, and Aaron T. Wolf, eds. *Water in the Middle East: A Geography of Peace.* (Austin: University of Texas Press, 2000), 227.

[46]Ibid.

[47]Ibid.

[48]Stephen McCaffrey, "The Harmon Doctrine One Hundred Years Later: Buried, Not Praised," *Natural Resources Journal* 136 (Summer 1996): 568.

[49]Rowley, "Political Controls of River Waters," 228.

[50]Wolf, "Hydropolitical History of the River Basins," 31.

[51]Rowley, "Political Controls of River Waters," 228.

[52]Shapland, *Rivers of Discord*, 143.

[53]Rowley, "Political Controls of River Waters," 230.

[54]William J. Cosgrove, "Water Security and Peace: A Synthesis of Studies prepared under the PCCP-Water for Peace process," http://www.unwater.org/wwd09/downloads/133318e.pdf (accessed February 28, 2012), 27.

[55]Rowley, "Political Controls of River Waters," 230, 231.

[56]Ibid, 231.

[57]*Convention on the Law of the Non-navigational Uses of International Watercourses*, General Assembly Resolution 51/229, United Nations (May 21, 1997), http://daccess-dds-ny.un.org/doc/UNDOC/GEN/N97/772/93/PDF/N9777293.pdf?OpenElement (accessed March 3, 2012), 4.

[58]Ibid, 5.

[59]Ibid.

[60]United Nations Bibliographic Information System (UBISNET), http://unbisnet.un.org:8080/ipac20/ipac.jsp?session=13308245RI575.513756&profile=voting&uri=full=3100023~!483283~!0&ri=1&aspect=power&menu=search&source=~!horizon&addkeys=bkey483283#focus (accessed March 3, 2012).

[61]United Nations Treaty Collection, "Chapter XXVII: Environment: 12. Convention on the Law of the Non-navigational Uses of International Watercourses," March 3, 2012, http://treaties.un.org/Pages/ViewDetails.aspx?src=TREATY&mtdsg_no=XXVII-12&chapter=27&lang=en (accessed March 3, 2012).

[62]"Statement by Mr. Celem (Turkey)," May 21, 1997, *United Nation Audiovisual Library of International Law*, http://untreaty.un.org/cod/avl/ha/clnuiw/clnuiw_video.html (accessed March 3, 2012).

[63]Republic of Turkey Ministry of Foreign Affairs, "Water: A source of conflict or cooperation in the Middle East?" http://www.mfa.gov.tr/data/DISPOLITIKA/WaterASourceofConflictofCoopintheMiddleEast.pdf (accessed March 3, 2012).

[64]Shapland, *Rivers of Discord*, 120.

[65]Ibid.

[66]United Nations Environment Program, "The World Commission on Dams," http://unep.org/dams/WCD (accessed March 3, 2012).

[67]*Dams and Development: A New Framework for Decision-Making: The Report of the World Commission on Dams*, (London: Earthscan Publications, 2000), http://unep.org/dams/WCD/report/WCD_DAMS%20report.pdf (accessed March 3, 2012), 174.

[68]Elizabeth Angell, "The Ilisu Dam's Uncertain Future," August 19, 2009 http://www.chinadialogue.net/article/show/single/en/3223-The-Ilisu-Dam-s-uncertain-future- (accessed February 15, 2012).

[69]Joe Gelt, "Sharing Colorado River Water: History, Public Policy and the Colorado River Compact," *Arroyo Online* 10, no. 1 (August 1997) http://ag.arizona.edu/azwater/arroyo/101comm.html (accessed March 4, 2012).

[70]Clarence Stetson, "Minutes of the 11th Meeting Colorado River Commission," November 11, 1922, http://wwa.colorado.edu/colorado_river/docs/compact/meeting11.pdf (accessed March 4, 2012).

[71]Gelt, "Sharing Colorado River Water."

[72]Ibid.

[73]"Colorado River Compact," November 24, 1922, http://wwa.colorado.edu/colorado_river/docs/CO%20River%20Compact.pdf (accessed March 4, 2012), 2.

[74]Charles J. Meyers and Richard L. Noble, "The Colorado River: The Treaty With Mexico," *Stanford Law Review* 19, no. 2 (January 1967): 368, in JSTOR (accessed March 4, 2012).

[75]Treaty between the United States of America and Mexico, February 3, 1944, http://www.usbr.gov/lc/region/g1000/pdfiles/mextrety.pdf (accessed March 4, 2012), 10, 21.

[76]International Boundary and Water Commission, "United States and Mexico: Colorado River Boundary Section," http://www.ibwc.gov/Water_Data/Colorado/Index.html (accessed March 4, 2012).

[77]Trade and Environment Database, "Colorado River Water Dispute (Colorado Case)," http://www1.american.edu/TED/colorado.htm (accessed March 4, 2012).

[78]U.S. Water News Online, "Report delves into details of U.S., Mexico water treaty," November 2004, http://www.uswaternews.com/archives/arcglobal/4repodelv11.html (accessed March 3, 2012).

[79]Lolita Baldor and Rebecca Santanna, "US formally ends Iraq war with little fanfare," December 15, 2011, http://msnbc.com/id/45691156 (accessed January 13, 2012).

[80]Brahma Chellaney and Ashley J. Tellis, "A Crisis to Come? China, India, and Water Rivalry," September 13, 2011, http://carnegieendowment.org/2011/09/13/crisis-to-come-china-india-and-water-rivalry/50nw (accessed March 4, 2011).

[81]Defense Intelligence Agency, "Iraqi Water Treatment Vulnerabilities," January 22, 1991, http://www.gulflink.osd.mil/declassdocs/dia/19950901/950901_511rept_91.html (accessed March 9, 2012).

[82]United Nations Food and Agriculture Organization, Country water briefs for Syria and Iraq, January 19, 2012,

http://www.fao.org/nr/water/aquastat/data/wbsheets/aquastat_water_balance_sheet_syr_en.pdf, http://www.fao.org/nr/water/aquastat/data/wbsheets/aquastat_water_balance_sheet_irq_en.pdf (accessed January 19, 2012).

[83]Defense Intelligence Agency, "Iraqi Water Treatment Vulnerabilities."

[84]NGO Coordination Committee in Iraq, "NCCI-OP-ED- Iraq Water Scarcity in the Land of Two Ancient Rivers," August 3, 2010, http://reliefweb.int/node/362880 (accessed March 9, 2012).

[85]IRIN humanitarian news and analysis, "Syria: Massive investment needed if Damascus to avert water crisis," October 11, 2006, http://www.irinnews.org/Report/61878/SYRIA-Massive-investment-needed-if-Damascus-to-avert-water-crisis (accessed March 9, 2012).

[86]Peter H. Gleick, Heather Cooley, and Gary Wolff, "With a Grain of Salt: An Update on Seawater Desalination," in *The World's Water, 2004-2005: The Biennial Report on Freshwater Resources* (Washington, DC: Island Press, 2004), 51.

[87]Ibid.

[88]Ibid, 52.

[89]Heather Cooley, "Tampa Bay Desalination Plant: An Update," in *The World's Water, 2008-2009: The Biennial Report on Freshwater Resources* (Washington, DC: Island Press, 2009), 124.

[90]Gleick, Cooley, and Wolff, "With a Grain of Salt," 70.

[91]Alex Prud'homme, *The Ripple Effect: The Fate of Freshwater in the Twenty-First Century* (New York: Scribner, 2011), 332.

[92]Gleick, Cooley, and Wolff, "With a Grain of Salt," 69, 72.

[93]"Two New Desalination Plants at Basra Ports," March 28, 2010, http://www.iraq-businessnews.com/2010/03/28/2-contracts-signed-to-establish-desalination-plants-in-basra-ports/ (accessed March 9, 2012).

[94]"Iraq buys solar desalination units," June 21, 2010, http://www.utilities-me.com/article-606-iraq-buys-solar-desalination-units/ (accessed March 9, 2012).

[95]Peter H. Gleick, *The World's Water, 2008-2009: The Biennial Report on Freshwater Resources* (Washington, DC: Island Press, 2009), xv, xvi.

[96]United Nations Food and Agriculture Organization, "Improving Irrigation Technology," March 2003, http://www.fao.org/ag/magazine/0303sp3.htm (accessed March 11, 2012).

[97]Prud'homme, *The Ripple Effect*, 251.

[98] Bretton Woods Project, "Farming furore: World Bank launches new agriculture fund," February 15, 2010, http://www.brettonwoodsproject.org/art-565915 (accessed March 11, 2012).

[99] The World Bank News and Broadcast, "World Bank reactivates food fund amid concern over food volatility," http://web.worldbank.org/WBSITE/EXTERNAL/NEWS/0,,contentMDK:22736243~pagePK:6425 7043~piPK:437376~theSitePK:4607,00.html (accessed March 11, 2012).